Design Direct

Breezy Duster page 2

Shell Cardigan page 8

Camisole Top page 12

Entwined Rings Belt page 15

Scallop Jacket page 16

Quick Accent Scarf page 20

Breezy Duster

INTERMEDIATE

Sizes

Woman's small [medium, large, X-large, 2X-large]
Pattern is written for smallest size with changes for larger sizes in brackets.

Finished Measurement

36 inches *(small)* [40 inches *(medium)*, 44 inches *(large)*, 48 inches *(X-large)*, 52 inches *(2X-large*]

Materials

- DMC Senso size 3 crochet cotton: 2,850 [3,150, 3,450, 3,750, 4,050] yds #1109 turquoise
- Size E/4/3.5mm crochet hook or size needed to obtain gauge
- Tapestry needle
- Stitch markers
- 40 assorted matching glass beads

Gauge

2 pattern reps = 5 inches

Instructions

Body

***Note:** Body is worked in 1 piece to armholes.*

Row 1 (RS): Ch 166 [190, 214, 238, 262]; 3 dc in 4th ch from hook *(beg 3 sk chs count as a dc)*—beg shell made; sk next 5 chs, 4 dc in next ch—shell made; *ch 4, sk next 2 chs, sc in next ch, ch 4, sk next 2 chs, 4 dc in next ch—shell made; sk next 5 chs, 4 dc in next ch—shell made; rep from * across, turn. *(28 [32, 36, 40, 44] shells)*

Row 2: Ch 3 *(counts as a dc on this and following rows),* 3 dc in first dc—beg shell made; *shell in 4th dc of next shell; ch 4, sc in next sc, ch 4, shell in first dc of next shell; rep from * to beg shell; shell in 3rd ch of beg 3 sk chs, turn.

Row 3: Ch 7 *(counts as a dc and a ch-4 sp on this and following rows);* *sc in sp between shells, ch 4, shell in 4th dc of next shell, shell in first dc of next shell; ch 4; rep from * to last shell; sc in sp between shells, ch 4, dc in 3rd ch of turning ch, turn.

Row 4: Ch 7; *sc in next sc, ch 4, shell in first dc of next shell, shell in 4th dc of next shell; ch 4; rep from * to last sc; sc in last sc, ch 4, dc in 3rd ch of turning ch-7, turn.

Row 5: Beg shell in first dc; *shell in first dc of next shell; ch 4, sc in sp between shells, ch 4, shell in 4th dc of next shell; rep from * to turning ch-7; shell in 3rd ch of turning ch-7, turn.

Rep Rows 2–5 until piece measures about 30 inches in length, ending with a row 4.

Right Front

For Sizes Small, Large & 2X-Large Only

Row 1: Beg shell in first dc; *shell in first dc of next shell, ch 4, sc in sp between shells, ch 4, shell in 4th dc of next shell; rep from * 2 [3, 4] times more; shell in first dc of next shell, turn, leaving rem sts unworked. *(8 [10, 12] shells)*

Row 2: Beg shell in first dc; *shell in 4th dc of next shell; ch 4, sc in next sc, ch 4, shell in first dc of next shell; rep from * to beg shell; shell in 3rd ch of turning ch-3, turn.

Row 3: Ch 7; *sc in sp between shells, ch 4, shell in 4th dc of next shell, shell in first dc of next shell; ch 4; rep from * to last shell; sc in sp between shells, ch 4, dc in 3rd ch of turning ch, turn.

Row 4: Ch 7; *sc in next sc, ch 4, shell in first dc of next shell, shell in 4th dc of next shell; ch 4; rep from * to last sc; sc in last sc, ch 4, dc in 3rd ch of turning ch-7, turn.

Row 5: Beg shell in first dc; *shell in first dc of next shell; ch 4, sc in sp between shells, ch 4, shell in 4th dc of next shell; rep from * to turning ch-7; shell in 3rd ch of turning ch-7, turn.

Rep rows 2–5 until armhole measures 5 [6, 7] inches.

Neck Shaping

Row 1: Beg shell in first dc; *shell in 4th dc of next shell, ch 4, sc in next sc, ch 4, shell in first dc of next shell; rep from * 1 [2, 3] times more; shell in 4th dc of next shell, turn, leaving rem sts unworked.

Row 2: Ch 7; *sc in sp between shells, ch 4, shell in 4th dc of next shell, shell in first dc of next shell; ch 4; rep from * to last shell; sc in sp between shells, ch 4, dc in 3rd ch of turning ch, turn.

Row 3: Ch 7; *sc in next sc, ch 4, shell in first dc of next shell, shell in 4th dc of next shell; ch 4; rep from * to last sc; sc in last sc, ch 4, dc in 3rd ch of turning ch-7, turn.

Row 4: Beg shell in first dc; *shell in first dc of next shell; ch 4, sc in sp between shells, ch 4, shell in 4th dc of next shell; rep from * to turning ch-7; shell in 3rd ch of turning ch, turn.

Row 5: Beg shell in first dc; *shell in 4th dc of next shell, ch 4, sc in next sc, ch 4, shell in first dc of next shell; rep from * 1 [3, 5] times more; 4 dc in 3rd ch of turning ch-3.

Rep rows 2–5 until armhole measures 8 [9, 10] inches. Fasten off.

Continue with Back.

For Sizes Medium & X-Large Only

Row 1: Beg shell in first dc; *shell in first dc of next shell, ch 4, sc in sp between shells, ch 4, shell in 4th dc of next shell; rep from * [3, 4] times more, turn, leaving rem sts unworked. *([9, 11] shells)*

Row 2: Beg shell in first dc; ch 4, sc in next sc, ch 4, shell in first dc of next shell; *shell in 4th dc of next shell; ch 4, sc in next sc, ch 4, shell in first dc of next shell; rep from * to beg shell; shell in 3rd ch of turning ch-3, turn.

Row 3: Ch 7; *sc in sp between shells, ch 4, shell in 4th dc of next shell, shell in first dc of next shell; ch 4; rep from * 2 [3] times more; sc in sp between shells, ch 4, shell in 4th dc of next shell, shell in first dc of next shell, turn.

Row 4: Beg shell in first dc; shell in 4th dc of next shell; ch 4; *sc in next sc, ch 4, shell in first dc of next shell, shell in 4th dc of next shell; ch 4; rep from * to last sc; sc in last sc, ch 4, dc in 3rd ch of turning ch-7, turn.

Row 5: Beg shell in first dc; *shell in first dc of next shell; ch 4, sc in sp between shells, ch 4, shell in 4th dc of next shell; rep from * to last shell; shell in first dc of last shell; ch 4, sc in sp between shells, ch 4, shell in 3rd ch of turning ch-3, turn.

Rep rows 2–5 until armhole measures [5½, 6½] inches.

Neck Shaping

Row 1: Beg shell in first dc; ch 4, sc in next sc, ch 4, shell in first dc of next shell; *shell in 4th dc of next shell; ch 4, sc in next sc, ch 4, shell in first dc of next shell; rep from * 1 [2] times more; shell in 4th ch of next shell, turn, leaving rem sts unworked.

Row 2: Ch 7; *sc in sp between shells, ch 4, shell in 4th dc of next shell, shell in first dc of next shell; ch 4, rep from * 1 [2] times more; ch 4, shell in 4th dc of next shell, shell in first dc of next shell, turn.

Row 3: Beg shell in first dc; shell in 4th dc of next shell; ch 4; *sc in next sc, ch 4, shell in first dc of next shell, shell in 4th dc of next shell; ch 4; rep from * to last sc; sc in last sc, ch 4, dc in 3rd ch of turning ch-7, turn.

Row 4: Beg shell in first dc; *shell in first dc of next shell; ch 4, sc in sp between shells, ch 4, shell in 4th dc of next shell; rep from * to last shell; shell in first dc of last shell; ch 4, sc in sp between shells, ch 4, dc in 3rd ch of turning ch-3, turn.

Row 5: Beg shell in first dc; ch 4, sc in next sc, ch 4, shell in first dc of next shell; *shell in 4th dc of next shell; ch 4, sc in next sc, ch 4, shell in first dc of next shell; rep from * 1 [2] times more; shell in 4th ch of next shell, turn.

Rep rows 2–5 until armhole measures [8½, 9½] inches. Fasten off.

Continue with Back.

Back

Hold piece with RS facing you; join crochet cotton in same dc as last shell of Right Front made.

Row 1 (RS): Ch 7; *sc in sp between shells, ch 4, shell in 4th dc of next shell; shell in first dc of next shell; ch 4; rep from * 5 [6, 7, 8, 9] times more; sc in sp between shells, ch 4, shell in 4th dc of next shell, turn, leaving rem sts unworked.

Row 2: Ch 7; *sc in next sc, ch 4, shell in first dc of next shell, shell in 4th dc of next shell; ch 4; rep from * to last sc; sc in last sc, ch 4, dc in 3rd ch of turning ch-7, turn.

Row 3: Beg shell in first dc; *shell in first dc of next shell; ch 4, sc in sp between shells, ch 4, shell in 4th dc of next shell; rep from * to turning ch-7; shell in 3rd ch of turning ch, turn.

Row 4: Beg shell in first dc; *shell in 4th dc of next shell; ch 4, sc in next sc, ch 4, shell in first dc of next shell; rep from * to beg shell; shell in 3rd ch of turning ch-3, turn.

Row 5: Ch 7; *sc in sp between shells, ch 4, shell in 4th dc of next shell, shell in first dc of next shell; ch 4; rep from * to last shell; sc in sp between shells, ch 4, dc in 3rd ch of turning ch, turn.

Rep rows 2–5 until back measures same as Right Front. Fasten off.

Continue with Left Front.

Left Front

For Sizes Small, Large & 2X-Large Only

Hold piece with RS facing you; join crochet cotton in top of last dc of last shell of Back.

Row 1: *Shell in first dc of next shell; ch 4, sc in sp between shells, ch 4, shell in 4th dc of next shell; rep from * 2 [3, 4] times more; shell in 3rd ch of turning ch-7, turn. *(7 [9, 11] shells)*

Row 2: Beg shell in first dc; *shell in 4th dc of next shell; ch 4, sc in next sc, ch 4, shell in first dc of next shell; rep from * to first shell; shell in 4th dc of first shell, turn.

Row 3: Ch 7, shell in 4th dc of first shell, shell in first dc of next shell; ch 4; *sc in sp between shells, ch 4, shell in 4th dc of next shell, shell in first dc of next shell; ch 4; rep from * to last shell; sc in sp between shells, ch 4, dc in 3rd ch of turning ch, turn.

Row 4: Ch 7; *sc in next sc, ch 4, shell in first dc of next shell, shell in 4th dc of next shell; ch 4; rep from * to last sc; sc in last sc, ch 4, dc in 3rd ch of turning ch-7, turn.

Row 5: Beg shell in first dc; ch 4, sc in sp between shells, ch 4, shell in 4th dc of next shell; *shell in first dc of next shell; ch 4, sc in sp between shells, ch 4, shell in 4th dc of next shell; rep from * to turning ch-7; shell in 3rd ch of turning ch, turn.

Rep rows 2–5 until armhole measures 5 [6, 7] inches, ending with a row 4.

Neck Shaping

Row 1: Beg shell in first dc; ch 4, sc in sp between shell, ch 4; *shell in 4th dc of next shell; shell in first dc of next shell; ch 4, sc in next sc, ch 4; rep from * 1 [2, 3] times more; dc in 4th dc of next shell, turn, leaving rem sts unworked.

Row 2: Ch 7; *sc in next sc, ch 4, shell in first dc of next shell; shell in 4th dc of next shell, ch 4; rep from * 1[2, 3] times more; sc in next sc, ch 4, dc in 3rd ch of turning ch, turn.

Row 3: Ch 7; *sc in next sc, ch 4, shell in first dc of next shell, shell in 4th dc of next shell; ch 4; rep from * to last sc; sc in last sc, ch 4, dc in 3rd ch of turning ch-7, turn.

Row 4: Beg shell in first dc; *shell in first dc of next shell; ch 4, sc in sp between shells, ch 4, shell in 4th dc of next shell; rep from * to turning ch-7; shell in 3rd ch of turning ch, turn.

Row 5: Beg shell in first dc; *shell in 4th dc of next shell, ch 4, sc in next sc, ch 4, shell in first dc of next shell; rep from * 1 [2, 3] times more; 4 dc in 3rd ch of turning ch-3.

Rep rows 2–5 until armhole measures 8 [9, 10] inches.

Fasten off and weave in ends.

Continue with Sleeve.

For Sizes Medium & X-Large Only

Hold piece with RS facing you; join crochet cotton in 4th dc of same shell as last shell of Back made.

Row 1: Beg shell in same dc; shell in first dc of next shell; ch 4; *sc in sp between shells, ch 4, shell in 4th dc of next shell; shell in first dc of next shell; ch 4; rep from * [1, 2] times more; sc in sp between shells, ch 4, shell in shell in 4th dc of next shell; shell in 3rd ch of turning ch-7, turn. *(8 [10] shells)*

Row 2: Beg shell in first dc; *shell in 4th dc of next shell; ch 4, sc in next sc, ch 4, shell in first dc of next shell; rep from * to beg shell; shell in 3rd ch of beg ch-3, turn.

Row 3: Ch 7; *sc in sp between shells, ch 4, shell in 4th dc of next shell, shell in first dc of next shell; ch 4; rep from * to last shell; sc in sp between shells, ch 4, dc in 3rd ch of turning ch, turn.

Row 4: Ch 7; *sc in next sc, ch 4, shell in first dc of next shell, shell in 4th dc of next shell; ch 4; rep from * to last sc; sc in last sc, ch 4, dc in 3rd ch of turning ch-7, turn.

Row 5: Beg shell in first dc; *shell in first dc of next shell; ch 4, sc in sp between shells, ch 4, shell in 4th dc of next shell; rep from * to turning ch-7; shell in 3rd ch of turning ch, turn.

Row 6: Beg shell in first dc; *shell in 4th dc of next shell; ch 4, sc in next sc, ch 4, shell in first dc of next shell; rep from * to beg shell; shell in 3rd ch of turning ch-3, turn.

Rep rows 3–6 until armhole measures [5½, 6½] inches, ending with a row 5.

Neck Shaping

Row 1: Beg shell in first dc; *shell in 4th dc of next shell, ch 4, sc in next sc, ch 4, shell in first dc of next shell; rep from * 1 [2] times more; 4 dc in 4th dc of next shell, turn, leaving rem sts unworked.

Row 2: Ch 7; *sc in sp between shells, ch 4, shell in 4th dc of next shell, shell in first dc of next shell; ch 4; rep from * to last shell; sc in sp between shells, ch 4, dc in 3rd ch of turning ch, turn.

Row 3: Ch 7; *sc in next sc, ch 4, shell in first dc of next shell, shell in 4th dc of next shell; ch 4; rep from * to last sc; sc in last sc, ch 4, dc in 3rd ch of turning ch-7, turn.

Row 4: Beg shell in first dc; *shell in first dc of next shell; ch 4, sc in sp between shells, ch 4, shell in 4th dc of next shell; rep from * to turning ch-7; shell in 3rd ch of turning ch, turn.

Row 5: Beg shell in first dc; *shell in 4th dc of next shell, ch 4, sc in next sc, ch 4, shell in first dc of next shell; rep from * 1 [2] times more; 4 dc in 3rd ch of turning ch-3.

Rep rows 2–5 until armhole measures [8½, 9½] inches.

Fasten off and weave in ends.

Continue with Sleeve.

Sleeve

Make 2.

Front Section

Row 1 (RS): Ch 46 [46, 46, 58, 58]; 3 dc in 4th ch from hook *(beg 3 sk chs count as a dc)*—beg shell made; sk next 5 chs, 4 dc in next ch—shell made; *ch 4, sk next 2 chs, sc in next ch, ch 4, sk next 2 chs, 4 dc in next ch—shell made; sk next 5 chs, 4 dc in next ch—shell made; rep from * across, turn. *(8 [8, 8, 10, 10] shells)*

Row 2: Ch 3 *(counts as a dc on this and following rows)*, 3 dc in first dc; *shell in 4th dc of next shell; ch 4, sc in next sc, ch 4, shell in first dc of next shell; rep from * to beg shell; shell in 3rd ch of beg 3 sk chs, turn.

Row 3: Ch 7 *(counts as a dc and a ch-4 sp on his and following rows)*; *sc in sp between shells, ch 4, shell in 4th dc of next shell, shell in first dc of next shell; ch 4; rep from * to last shell; sc in sp between shells, ch 4, dc in 3rd ch of turning ch, turn.

Row 4: Ch 7; *sc in next sc, ch 4, shell in first dc of next shell, shell in 4th dc of next shell; ch 4; rep from * to last sc; sc in last sc, ch 4, dc in 3rd ch of turning ch-7, turn.

Row 5: Ch 3, 3 dc in first dc; *shell in first dc of next shell; ch 4, sc in sp between shells, ch 4, shell in 4th dc of next shell; rep from * to turning ch-7; shell in 3rd ch of turning ch, turn.

Rep rows 2–5 until piece measures 17 [17½, 17½, 18, 18] inches. Fasten off.

Back Section

Row 1: Ch 5 [7, 13, 17, 23]; dc in 4th ch from hook *(beg 3 sk chs count as a dc)* and in each rem ch, turn. *(3 [5, 11, 15, 21] dc)*

For Size Small Only

Note: *On next row, mark center dc. On following rows, move marker up.*

Row 2: Ch 3 *(counts as a dc on this and following rnds),* dc in next dc and in 3rd ch of beg 3 sk chs, turn. Mark center dc.

Row 3: Ch 3, dc in first dc, dc in next dc, 2 dc in 3rd ch of turning ch-3, turn. *(5 dc)*

Row 4: Ch 3, dc in each dc and in 3rd ch of turning ch-3, turn.

Row 5: Ch 3, 2 dc in next dc; dc in next marked dc, 2 dc in next dc; dc in 3rd ch of turning ch-3, turn. *(7 dc)*

Row 6: Rep row 4.

Row 7: Ch 3, dc in each dc to dc before marked dc; 2 dc in next dc; dc in marked dc, 2 dc in next dc; dc in each rem dc and in 3rd ch of turning ch-3, turn. *(9 dc)*

Rows 8–31: [Work rows 6 and 7] 12 times. *(33 dc)*

Rep row 6 until piece measures same as Front Section.

Fasten off and weave in ends.

For Size Medium Only

Note: *On next row, mark center dc. On following rows, move marker up.*

Row 2: Ch 3 *(counts as a dc on this and following rnds),* 2 dc in next dc; dc in next dc, 2 dc in next dc; dc in 3rd ch of beg 3 sk chs, turn. *(7 dc)*

Row 3: Ch 3, dc in each dc and in 3rd ch of turning ch-3, turn.

Row 4: Ch 3, dc in each dc to dc before marked dc; 2 dc in next dc; dc in marked dc, 2 dc in next dc; dc in each rem dc and in 3rd ch of turning ch-3, turn. *(9 dc)*

Rows 5–30: [Work rows 3 and 4] 13 times. *(35 dc)*

Rep row 3 until piece measures same as Front Section.

Fasten off and weave in ends.

For Size Large Only

Note: *On next row, mark center dc. On following rows, move marker up.*

Row 2: Ch 3 *(counts as a dc on this and following rnds),* dc in next 5 dc, 2 dc in next dc; dc in next dc, 2 dc in next dc; dc in next 4 dc and in 3rd ch of beg 3 sk chs, turn. *(13 dc)*

Row 3: Ch 3, dc in each dc and in 3rd ch of turning ch-3, turn.

Row 4: Ch 3, dc in each dc to dc before marked dc; 2 dc in next dc; dc in marked dc, 2 dc in next dc; dc in each rem dc and in 3rd ch of turning ch-3, turn. *(15 dc)*

Rows 5–30: [Work rows 3 and 4] 13 times. *(41 dc)*

Rep row 3 until piece measures same as Front Section.

Fasten off and weave in ends.

For Size X-Large Only

Note: *On next row, mark center dc. On following rows, move marker up.*

Row 2: Ch 3 *(counts as a dc on this and following rnds),* dc in next 7 dc, 2 dc in next dc; dc in next dc, 2 dc in next dc; dc in next 6 dc and in 3rd ch of beg 3 sk chs, turn. *(17 dc)*

Row 3: Ch 3, dc in each dc and in 3rd ch of turning ch-3, turn.

Row 4: Ch 3, dc in each dc to dc before marked dc; 2 dc in next dc; dc in marked dc, 2 dc in next dc; dc in each rem dc and in 3rd ch of turning ch-3, turn. *(19 dc)*

Rows 5–30: [Work rows 3 and 4] 13 times. *(45 dc)*

Rep row 3 until piece measures same as Front Section.

Fasten off and weave in ends.

For Size 2X-Large Only

Note: *On next row, mark center dc. On following rows, move marker up.*

Row 2: Ch 3 *(counts as a dc on this and following rnds),* dc in next 10 dc, 2 dc in next dc; dc in next dc, 2 dc in next dc; dc in next 9 dc and in 3rd ch of beg 3 sk chs, turn. *(23 dc)*

Row 3: Ch 3, dc in each dc and in 3rd ch of turning ch-3, turn.

Row 4: Ch 3, dc in each dc to dc before marked dc; 2 dc in next dc; dc in marked dc, 2 dc in next dc; dc in each rem dc and in 3rd ch of turning ch-3, turn. *(25 dc)*

Rows 5–30: [Work rows 3 and 4] 13 times. *(51 dc)*

Rep row 3 until piece measures same as Front Section.

Fasten off and weave in ends.

Assembly

Sew shoulders tog. For Sleeves, sew Front Sections to Back Sections.

Sleeve Border

Hold 1 sleeve with beg ch at top; join crochet cotton in seam.

Rnd 1: Ch 1, sc in same sp and in each st; join in first sc.

Note: *Place 4 [4, 4, 5, 5] markers around last rnd, evenly spaced.*

Rnd 2: Ch 4 *(counts as a dc and a ch-1 sp),* dc in same st as joining—beg V-st made; sk next sc, in next st work (dc, ch 1, dc)—V-st made; work 3 more V-sts to marker, skipping sts as necessary; work 5 V-sts between each pair of rem markers; join in 3rd ch of beg ch-4. *(20 [20, 20, 25, 25] V-sts)*

Rnd 3: Ch 1, sc in same ch as joining; ch 5; *sc in ch-1 sp of next V-st, ch 5; rep from * around; join in first sc.

Rnd 4: Sl st in next ch-5 sp, ch 3 *(counts as a dc),* 3 dc in same sp; *[sc in next ch-5 sp, ch 5] 3 times; sc in next ch-5 sp, 8 dc in next ch-5 sp—shell made; rep from * 2 [3, 3, 3, 3] times more; [sc in next ch-5 sp, ch 5] 3 times; sc in next ch-5 sp, 4 dc in beg ch-5 sp, join in 3rd ch of beg ch-3.

Rnd 5: Ch 4 *(counts as a dc and a ch-1 sp),* [dc in next dc, ch 1] 3 times; dc in next dc; *[sc in next ch-5 sp, ch 5] twice; sc in next ch-5 sp, [dc in next dc, ch 1] 6 times; dc in next dc; rep from * 2 [3, 3, 3, 3] times more; [sc in next ch-5 sp, ch 5] twice; sc in next ch-5 sp, [dc in next dc, ch 1] 4 times; join in 3rd ch of beg ch-4.

Rnd 6: Ch 5 *(counts as a dc and a ch-2 sp),* [dc, ch 2] 3 times; dc in next dc; *sc in next ch-5 sp, ch 5, sc in next ch-5 sp, [dc in next dc, ch 2] 7 times; dc in next dc; rep from * 2 [3, 3, 3, 3] times more; sc in next ch-5 sp, ch 5, sc in next ch-5 sp, [dc in next dc, ch 2] 4 times; join in 3rd ch of beg ch-5.

Rnd 7: Sl st in next ch-2 sp, ch 6, sl st in 3rd ch from hook—beg picot made; [dc in next ch-2 sp, ch 3, sl st in 3rd ch from hook—picot made] twice; *sc in next ch-5 sp, picot, [dc in next ch-2 sp, picot] 7 times; rep from * twice more; sc in next ch-5 sp, picot; joining in base of beg picot.

Fasten off and weave in ends.

Rep on other sleeve.

Finishing

Sew in Sleeves.

Body Border

Join crochet cotton in 1 shoulder seam.

Rnd 1: Ch 1, sc evenly spaced around outer edge of duster and working 3 sc in each corner; join in first sc.

Note: *Remainder of border is based on a multiple of 5 V-sts. As you work, place marker on each 5th V-st (moving marker as you work 5 more V-sts) so sts can be adjusted to meet the required multiple of 5 V-sts.*

Rnd 2: Ch 4 *(counts as a dc and a ch-1 sp),* dc in same st as joining—beg V-st made; *sk next sc, V-st in next st; rep from * working 1 V-st in each of 3 sc at each corner; join in 3rd ch of beg ch-4.

Rnd 3: Ch 1, sc in same ch as joining; *ch 5, sc in ch-1 sp of next V-st; rep from * around; ch 5; join in first sc.

Rnd 4: Sl st in next ch-5 sp, ch 3 *(counts as a dc),* 3 dc in same sp; [sc in next ch-5 sp, ch-5] 3 times; sc in next ch-5 sp; *8 dc in next ch-5 sp—shell made; [sc in next ch-5 sp, ch-5] 3 times; sc in next ch-5 sp; rep from * to beg ch-5 sp; 4 dc in beg ch-5 sp, join in 3rd ch of beg ch-3.

Rnd 5: Ch 4 *(counts as a dc and a ch-1 sp),* [dc in next dc, ch 1] 3 times; dc in next dc; [sc in next ch-5 sp, ch 5] twice; sc in next ch-5 sp; *[dc in next dc, ch 1] 6 times; dc in next dc, [sc in next ch-5 sp, ch 5] twice; sc in next ch-5 sp; rep from * to beg ch-4; join in 3rd ch of beg ch-4.

Rnd 6: Ch 5 *(counts as a dc and a ch-2 sp),* [dc, ch 2] 3 times; dc in next dc; sc in next ch-5 sp, ch 5, sc in next ch-5 sp; *[dc in next dc, ch 2] 7 times; dc in next dc, sc in next ch-5 sp, ch 5, sc in next ch-5 sp; rep from * to beg ch-5; join in 3rd ch of beg ch-5.

Rnd 7: Sl st in next ch-2 sp, ch 6, sl st in 3rd ch from hook—beg picot made; [dc in next ch-2 sp, ch 3, sl st in 3rd ch from hook—picot made] twice; sc in next ch-5 sp, picot; *[dc in next ch-2 sp, picot] 7 times; sc in next ch-5 sp, picot; rep from * to beg ch-6; joining in base of beg picot.

Fasten off and weave in ends.

Beaded Ties

Front Ties

For Ties, cut 2 (3-yd) lengths of crochet cotton. Thread 11 beads on each length. Fold in half forming lp with beads. Beg above beads, ch to end. Sew ends to front neck edges.

Sleeve Ties

For Ties, cut 2 (3-yd) lengths of crochet cotton. Thread 9 beads on each length. Fold in half forming lp with beads. Beg above beads, ch to end. Thread Tie through V-sts of Sleeve Border, placing bead lp at front of Sleeve. Knot on WS.

Shell Cardigan

EASY

Sizes

Woman's small [medium, large, X-large, 2X-large]
Pattern is written for smallest size with changes for larger sizes in brackets.

Finished Garment Measurements

36 inches *(small)* [40 inches *(medium)*, 44 inches *(large)*, 48 inches *(X-large)*, 52 inches *(2X-large*]

Materials

- DMC Senso Microfiber size 3 crochet cotton:
  1,800 [2,250, 2,700, 3,150, 3,600] yds #1001 white *(A)*
  300 [300, 300, 300, 300] yds #1109 turquoise *(B)*
  150 [150, 300, 300, 300] yds #1107 lime green *(C)*
- Sizes D/3/3.25mm and E/4/3.5mm crochet hooks or sizes needed to obtain gauge
- Tapestry needle
- 2 glass pendants

Gauge

With E hook: 4 shells = 5 inches

Special Stitch

Cross-stitch (X-st): Dc in sp between sc indicated and next dc, ch 1, dc in sp before same sc.

Instructions

Body

Note: *Body is worked in 1 piece to armholes. To change color, work last st until 2 lps rem on hook; with new color, yo and draw lp through 2 lps on hook. Cut old color.*

Row 1 (RS): With E hook and B, ch 183 [207, 219, 243, 267]; 2 dc in 4th ch from hook *(beg 3 sk chs count as a dc);* sk next ch, sc in next ch, sk next 2 chs; *5 dc in next ch—shell made; sk next 2 chs, sc in next ch, sk next 2 chs; rep from * to last ch; 3 dc in last ch, changing to A in last dc, turn. *(29 [33, 35, 39, 43] shells)*

Row 2: Ch 1, sc in first dc; *ch 1, **X-st** *(see Special Stitch)* in sps before and after next sc; ch 1, sc in 3rd dc of next shell; rep from * to last sc; ch 1, X-st in sps before and after last sc; ch 1, sc in 3rd ch of beg 3 sk chs, turn.

Row 3: Ch 1, sc in first sc, ch 1, sk next ch-1 sp, shell in ch-1 sp of next X-st; *ch 1, sk next 2 ch-1 sps, shell in ch-1 sp of next X-st; rep from * to last sc; ch 1, sc in last sc, changing to C, turn.

Row 4: Ch 3, dc in first sc; *ch 1, sc in 3rd dc of next shell, ch 1, X-st in sps before and after next sc on 2nd row below; rep from * to last shell; ch 1, sc in 3rd dc of last shell, ch 1, 2 dc in next sc, turn.

Row 5: Ch 3, 2 dc in first dc; *ch 1, shell in ch-1 sp of next X-st; rep from * to turning ch-3; ch 1, 3 dc in 3rd ch of turning ch-3, changing to A in last dc, turn.

Row 6: Ch 1, sc in first dc; *ch 1, X-st in sps before and after next sc on 2nd row below; ch 1, sc in 3rd dc of next shell; rep from * to last sc on 2nd row below; ch 1, X-st in sps before and after last sc on 2nd row below; ch 1, sc in 3rd ch of turning ch-3, turn.

Row 7: Ch 1, sc in first sc, ch 1, sk next ch-1 sp, shell in ch-1 sp of next X-st; *ch 1, sk next 2 ch-1 sps, shell in ch-1 sp of next X-st; rep from * to last sc; ch 1, sc in last sc, changing to B, turn.

Rep rows 4–7 in following color sequence until piece measures 11½ inches, ending with a RS row 7.

2 rows B

2 rows A

2 rows C

2 rows A

Next row (WS): Ch 1, hdc in first sc; *dc in next ch-1 sp, hdc in next dc, sc in next 3 dc, hdc in next dc, dc in next ch-1 sp, hdc in next dc; rep from * to last ch-1 sp; dc in last ch-1 sp, hdc in last sc; change to D hook, turn. *(182 [206, 218, 242, 266] sts)*

Right Front

Row 1 (RS): Ch 3; *sk next st, 2 dc in next st—V-st made; rep from* 21 [23, 25, 27, 29] times more; sk next st, dc in next st, turn, leaving rem sts unworked. *(46 [50, 54, 58, 62] dc)*

Row 2: Ch 3; V-st in sp between 2 dc of each V-st, dc in 3rd ch of turning ch-3, turn.

Row 3: Ch 2, dc in next dc and in sp between same dc and next dc, V-st in each rem V-st; dc in 3rd ch of turning ch-3. *(45 [49, 53, 57, 61] dc)*

Note: *For* ***dc dec,*** *[yo, insert in st indicated, draw lp through, yo, draw through 2 lps on hook] twice; yo and draw through all 3 lps on hook.*

Row 4: Ch 3, V-st in each V-st; **dc dec** *(see Note)* in next 2 dc, turn, leaving turning ch-2 unworked. *(44 [48, 52, 56, 60] dc)*

Rows 5–18: [Work rows 3 and 4] 7 times. *(30 [34, 38, 42, 46] dc at end of row 18)*

For Sizes Small, Medium & Large

Row 19: Ch 3; V-st in each V-st; dc in 3rd ch of turning ch-3, turn.

Rep row 19 until armhole measures 8 [8½, 9] inches from row 1. Fasten off.

Continue with Back.

Size X-Large & 2X-Large

Rows 19 & 20: Rep rows 3 and 4. *([40, 44] dc at end of row 20)*

Row 21: Ch 3; V-st in each V-st; dc in 3rd ch of turning ch-3, turn.

Rep row 21 until armhole measures [9½, 10] inches from row 1. Fasten off.

Continue with Back.

Back

Hold piece with RS facing you; with D hook, join A in next unused st on last row of Body from Right Front.

Row 1: Ch 3; *sk next st, V-st in next st; rep from * 42 [49, 52, 60, 66] times more; dc in next st, turn, leaving rem sts unworked. *(43 [50, 53, 61, 67] V-sts)*

Row 2: Ch 3, V-st in each V-st; dc in 3rd ch of beg ch-3, turn.

Row 3: Ch 3, V-st in each V-st; dc in 3rd ch of turning ch-3, turn.

Rep row 3 until armhole measures 8 [8½, 9, 9½, 10] inches. Fasten off.

Left Front

Hold piece with RS facing you; join A in next unused st on last row of Body from Back.

Row 1 (RS): Ch 3; *sk next st, V-st in next st; rep from * 21 [24, 25, 27, 29] times more; sk next dc, dc in next hdc, turn. *(46 [50, 54, 58, 62] dc)*

Row 2: Ch 3, V-st in each V-st; dc in 3rd ch of beg ch-3.

Row 3: Ch 3, V-st in each V-st to last V-st; dc dec in next V-st and in 3rd ch of beg ch-3, turn. *(45 [49, 53, 57, 61] dc)*

Row 4: Ch 3, V-st in each V-st; dc in 3rd ch of turning ch-3. *(44 [48, 52, 56, 60] dc)*

Rows 5–18: [Work rows 3 and 4] 5 times. *(30 [34, 38, 42, 46] dc at end of row 18)*

For Sizes Small, Medium & Large Only

Row 19: Ch 3; V-st in each V-st; dc in 3rd ch of turning ch-3, turn.

Rep row 19 until armhole measures 8 [8½, 9] inches from row 1. Fasten off.

Continue with Sleeve.

Size X-Large & 2X-Large Only

Rows 19 & 20: Rep rows 3 and 4. *([40, 44] dc at end of row 20)*

Row 21: Ch 3; V-st in each V-st; dc in 3rd ch of turning ch-3, turn.

Rep row 21 until armhole measures [9½, 10] inches from row 1. Fasten off.

Continue with Sleeve.

Sleeve

Make 2.

Row 1 (RS): With E hook and B, ch 52 [52, 52, 58, 58]; 2 dc in 4th ch from hook; sk next 2 chs, sc in next ch, sk next 2 chs; *5 dc in next ch—shell made; sk next 2 chs, sc in next ch, sk next 2 chs; rep from * to last ch; 3 dc in last ch; change to A, turn. *(7 [7, 7, 8, 8] shells)*

Row 2: Ch 1, sc in first dc; *ch 1, X-st in sps before and after next sc; ch 1, sc in 3rd dc of next shell; rep from * to last sc; ch 1, X-st in sps before and after last sc, ch 1, sc in 3rd ch of beg 3 sk chs, turn.

Row 3: Ch 1, sc in first sc, ch 1; *shell in ch-1 sp of next X-st; ch 1; rep from * to last X-st; shell in ch-1 sp of last X-st, sc in next sc; change to C, turn.

Row 4: Ch 3, dc in first sc; *ch 1, sc in 3rd dc of next shell, ch 1, X-st in sps before and after next sc on 2nd row below; rep from * to last shell; ch 1, sc in 3rd dc of last shell, ch 1, 2 dc in next sc, turn.

Row 5: Ch 3, 2 dc in first dc; *ch 1, shell in ch-1 sp of next X-st; rep from * turning ch-3; ch 1, 3 dc in 3rd ch of turning ch; change to A, turn.

Row 6: Ch 1, sc in first dc; *ch 1, X-st in sps before and after next sc on 2nd row below; ch 1, sc in 3rd dc of next shell; rep from * to last sc on 2nd row below; ch 1, X-st in sps before and after last sc on 2nd row below; ch 1, sc in 3rd ch of turning ch-3, turn.

Row 7: Ch 1, sc in first sc, ch 1, sk next ch-1 sp, shell in ch-1 sp of next X-st; *ch 1, sk next 2 ch-1 sps, shell in ch-1 sp of next X-st; rep from * to last sc; ch 1, sc in last sc, changing to B, turn.

Row 8: Ch 1, hdc in first sc; *dc in next ch-1 sp, hdc in next dc, sc in next 3 dc, hdc in next dc, dc in next ch-1 sp, hdc in next dc; rep from * to last ch-1 sp; dc in last ch-1 sp, hdc in last sc; change to D hook, turn. *(51 [51, 51, 57, 57] sts)*

Row 9: Ch 3, dc in first hdc; *sk next st, V-st in next st; rep from * to last 2 sts; sk next st, 2 dc in last st, turn. *(52 [52, 52, 58, 58] sts)*

Row 10: Ch 3, dc in next dc, V-st in sp between 2 dc of each V-st; sk last dc of last V-st, dc in next dc and in 3rd ch of turning ch-3.

Row 11: Ch 3, dc in first dc and in next dc; V-st in each V-st; sk last dc of last V-st, dc in next dc, 2 dc in 3rd ch of turning ch-3, turn. *(54 [54, 54, 60, 60] dc)*

Row 12: Ch 3, dc in next 2 dc, V-st in each V-st; sk last dc of last V-st, dc in next 2 dc and in 3rd ch of turning ch-3.

Row 13: Ch 3, dc in first; V-st in sp between next 2 dc; V-st in each V-st; sk last dc of last V-st, V-st in sp between next 2 dc; 2 dc in 3rd ch of turning ch-3, turn. *(56 [56, 56, 62, 62] dc)*

Row 14: Ch 3, dc in next dc, V-st in each V-st; sk last dc of last V-st, dc in next dc and in 3rd ch of turning ch-3.

For Sizes Small, X-Large & 2X-Large Only

Rows 15–38 [15–54, 15–58]: [Work rows 11–14] 6 [10, 11] times. *(80 [96,100] dc at end of last row)*

Row 39 [55, 59]: Ch 3, dc in next dc, V-st in each V-st; sk last dc of last V-st, dc in next dc and in 3rd ch of turning ch-3.

Rep row 39 [55, 59] until piece measures 17 [18, 18] inches.

Fasten off and weave in all ends.

Continue with Finishing.

For Size Medium & Large Only

Rows [15–42, 15–46]: [Work rows 11–14] [7, 8] times.

Rows [43 & 44, 47 & 48]: Work rows 11 and 12.

Row [45, 49]: Ch 3, dc in next 2 dc, V-st in each V-st; sk last dc of last V-st, dc in next 2 dc and in 3rd ch of turning ch-3.

Rep row [45, 49] until piece measures [17½, 17½] inches.

Continue with Finishing

Finishing

Sew shoulder seams. Sew Sleeve seams. Sew in Sleeves.

Edgings

Sleeve Edging

With D hook, join B in 1 seam; ch 1, sc in same sp; sc evenly spaced to first sc; join in first sc.

Fasten off and weave in ends.

Rep on other sleeve.

Lower Edging

Hold cardigan with RS facing you and beg ch at top; with D hook, join B in unused lp of first ch in upper right-hand corner; ch 1, sc in same lp; working across side in unused lps and in chs, sc in each st.

Fasten off and weave in ends.

Front Edging

Note: *For* ***sc dec,*** *draw up lp in each st indicated, yo and draw through all 3 lps on hook.*

Hold cardigan with RS facing you and Right Front edge at top; with D hook, join A in edge of row 1.

Row 1: Ch 1, sc in same sp; working across side in ends of rows, sc evenly spaced to first row of neck shaping; 3 sc in first row; working along neck edge, sc evenly spaced to shoulder seam; working across last row of Back, ***sc in next 2 sc, **sc dec** *(see Note)* in next 2 sc; rep from * to next shoulder seam; working across neck edge, sc evenly spaced to first row of neck shaping; 3 sc in first row; working across Left Front edge, sc evenly spaced to Row 1, turn.

Row 2: Ch 1, sc in each sc, turn.

Row 3: Ch 1, sc in each sc.

Fasten off and weave in ends.

Tie

Make 2.

Cut 2 (1-yd) lengths of A for each pendant. Thread through pendant, fold crochet cotton in half with pendant at center, make slip knot and sc to end. Sew ties to front neck edges.

Camisole Top

EASY

Sizes

Woman's small [medium, large, X-large] Pattern is written for smallest size with changes for larger sizes in brackets.

Finished Measurement

36 inches *(small)* [40 inches *(medium)*, 44 inches *(large)*, 48 inches *(X-large)*]

Materials

- J. & P. Coats Royale size 3 crochet cotton: 1,050 [1,200, 1,350, 1,650] yds #325 tangerine
- Size D/3/3.25mm crochet hook or size needed to obtain gauge
- Tapestry needle
- 2 gold ½-inch-diameter shank ball buttons

Gauge

5 dc = 1 inch

Instructions

Back

Row 1 (RS): Ch 93 [109, 117, 125]; in 7th ch from hook work (4 dc, ch 2, dc)—shell made *(beg 6 sk chs count as a ch-1 sp, a dc and a ch-1 sp);* *sk next 3 chs, in next ch work (dc, ch 1, 1 dc)—V-st made; sk next 3 chs, in next ch work (4 dc, ch 2, dc)—shell made; rep from * to last 6 chs; sk next 3 chs, in next ch work (dc, ch 1, dc)—V-st made; sk next ch, dc in last ch, turn.

Row 2: Ch 3; *V-st in ch-1 sp of next V-st, shell in ch-2 sp of next shell; rep from * to beg 6 sk chs, sk next ch, dc in next ch, turn.

Row 3: Ch 3; *shell in ch-2 sp of next shell; V-st in ch-1 sp of next V-st; rep from * to turning ch-3; dc in 3rd ch of turning ch, turn.

Rep rows 2 and 3 until piece measures 10 inches in length, ending with a row 3.

Upper Back

Row 1: Ch 3; *dc in next dc, sk next ch-1 sp, dc in next 2 dc, in next ch-2 sp and in next 4 dc; rep from * across, turn, leaving turning ch unworked. *(89 [105, 113, 121] dc)*

Row 2: Ch 4 *(counts as a dc and a ch-1 sp);* *sk next dc, dc in next st, ch 1; rep from * to turning ch-3; dc in 3rd ch of turning ch, turn.

Row 3: Ch 3; dc in each dc and in each ch-1 sp, turn. *(89 [105, 113, 121] dc)*

Row 4: Ch 3, dc in each dc and in 3rd ch of turning ch-3, turn.

Rep row 4 until piece measures about 4½ inches above row 2, ending with a RS row. Fasten off.

Armhole Shaping

Hold piece with WS facing you; sk first 7 [13, 14, 16] sts of last row worked; join in next dc.

Row 1: Ch 3, dc in next 74 [78, 84, 88] dc, turn, leaving last 7 [13, 14, 16] sts unworked. *(75 [79, 85, 89] dc)*

Note: *For* ***dc dec,*** *[yo, insert hook in st indicated, draw lp through, yo, draw through 2 lps on hook] twice; yo and draw through all 3 lps on hook.*

Row 2: Ch 3; **dc dec** *(see Note)* over next 2 sts, dc in each dc to last 3 sts; dc dec over next 2 sts, dc in 3rd ch of turning ch-3, turn. *(73 [77, 83, 87] dc)*

Row 3: Ch 3, dc in each dc and in 3rd ch of turning ch-3, turn.

Row 4: Ch 3; dc dec; dc in each dc to last 3 dc; dc dec; dc in 3rd ch of turning ch-3, turn. *(71 [75, 81, 85] dc)*

Row 5: Ch 3, dc in each dc and in 3rd ch of turning ch-3, turn.

Row 6: Ch 3; dc dec; dc in each dc to last 3 sts; dc dec; dc in 3rd ch of turning ch-3, turn. *(69 [73, 79, 83] dc)*

Rep row 5 until armhole measures 4 [4½, 5, 5½] inches, ending with a WS row.

Right Shoulder Shaping

Row 1: Ch 3, dc in next 14 [16, 18, 19] dc, turn, leaving rem sts unworked. *(15 [17, 19, 20] dc)*

Row 2: Ch 3, dc in each dc and in 3rd ch of turning ch-3, turn.

Rep row 2 until armhole measures 8 [8½, 9, 9½] inches. Fasten off.

Left Shoulder Shaping

Hold piece with RS facing you; sk next 39 [41, 43, 45] dc from Right Shoulder Shaping. Attach crochet cotton to next st.

Row 1: Ch 3, dc in next 13 [15, 17, 18] dc and in 3rd ch of turning ch-3, turn. *(15 [17, 19, 20] dc)*

Row 2: Ch 3, dc in each dc and in 3rd ch of turning ch-3, turn.

Rep row 2 until armhole measures 8 [8½, 9, 9½] inches.

Fasten off.

Front

Work as for Back through Armhole Shaping.

Last row: Ch 3, dc in each dc and in 3rd ch of turning ch-3, turn.

Right Shoulder Shaping

Row 1 (WS): Ch 3; dc in next 17 [18, 20, 21] dc, dc dec; dc in next dc, turn, leaving rem sts unworked.

Row 2 (RS): Ch 3; dc in each dc and in 3rd ch of turning ch-3 turn.

Row 3: Ch 3, dc in each dc to last 3 sts; dc dec; dc in 3rd ch of turning ch-3, turn.

Rows 4–11: [Rep rows 2 and 3] 5 times. *(15 [16, 18, 19] dc)*

Rep row 2 until piece measures same as back to shoulder. Fasten off.

Left Shoulder Shaping

Hold piece with WS facing you; sk next 27 [29, 31, 33] dc from Right Shoulder Shaping; join in next dc.

Row 1: Ch 3, dc dec; dc in next 17 [18, 20, 21] dc and in 3rd ch of turning ch-3, turn. *(20 (21, 23, 24] dc)*

Row 2: Ch 3, dc in each dc and in 3rd ch of turning ch-3, turn.

Row 3: Ch 3, dc dec; dc in each rem dc and in 3rd ch of turning ch-3, turn. *(19 (20, 22, 23] dc)*

Rows 4–11: [Rep rows 2 and 3] 5 times. *(15 (16, 18, 19] dc)*

Rep row 2 until piece measures same as right shoulder. Fasten off.

Assembly

With RS facing you, sew shoulder seams and side seams.

Edgings

Armhole Edging

Hold piece with RS facing you; join crochet cotton in 1 underarm seam; ch 1, sc in same sp; sc evenly spaced around armhole; join in first sc. Fasten off.

Rep on other armhole.

Lower Edging

Hold piece with RS facing you and lower edge at top; join crochet cotton in 1 side seam.

Rnd 1: Ch 1, sc in same sp; working in unused lps of beg ch, sc in each lp and in next seam; join in first sc.

Rnd 2: Ch 3 *(counts as a dc),* 2 dc in same sc; 3 dc in each rem sc; join in 3rd ch of beg ch 3. Fasten off.

Neck Edging

Hold piece with RS facing you; join crochet cotton in 1 shoulder seam.

Rnd 1: Ch 1, sc in same sp; sc evenly spaced around neck edge, taking care to keep work flat; join in first sc.

Rnd 2: Ch 3 *(counts as a dc),* 2 dc in same sc; 3 dc in each rem sc; join in 3rd ch of beg ch-3.

Fasten off and weave in all ends.

Tie

Make ch about 1¾ yds in length or desired length. Fasten off and weave in ends.

Finishing

Beg at center of front, thread tie through row 2 of Upper Front and Upper Back. Attach 1 ball button to each end of Tie. Tie into bow.

Entwined Rings Belt

EASY

Size

1½ x 25½ inches

Materials

- J. & P. Coats Royale size 3 crochet cotton: 150 yds each #175 warm blue and #926 bridal white
- Size E/4/3.5mm crochet hook or size needed to obtain gauge
- Tapestry needle
- 2-inch belt buckle
- Sewing needle and matching thread

Gauge

1 ring = 1¾ inches in diameter

Instructions

First Ring

With warm blue, ch 10; join to form a ring; ch 3 *(counts as a dc)*, 23 dc in ring; join in 3rd ch of beg ch-3.

Fasten off and weave in ends.

Second Ring

With bridal white, ch 10; insert end in completed ring; join to form a ring; ch 3 *(counts as a dc)*, 23 dc in ring; join in 3rd ch of beg ch3.

Fasten off and weave in ends.

Additional Ring

Alternating colors, work 21 Additional Rings in same manner as Second Ring or as many as needed for desired length.

Finishing

Sew ends to belt buckle. If desired, tack rings to each other on WS of work to avoid twisting.

Scallop Jacket

EASY

Sizes

Woman's small [medium, large, X-large] Pattern is written for smallest size with changes for larger sizes in brackets.

Finished Measurement

36 inches *(small)* [40 inches *(medium)*, 44 inches *(large)*, 48 inches *(X-large)*]

Materials

- DMC Senso Microfiber size 3 crochet cotton: 750 [900, 1,050, 1,200] yds #1105 medium pink *(A)* 300 [300, 450, 450] yds #1104 light pink *(B)*
- Size E/4/3.5mm crochet hook or size needed to obtain gauge
- Size D/3/3.25mm crochet hook
- Tapestry needle
- 2 jewelry charms, optional

3 LIGHT

Gauge

5 dc = 1 inch

Instructions

Body

Row 1 (RS): With E hook and B, ch 177 [201, 225, 249]; 5 dc in 6th ch from hook—shell made; sk next 2 chs, dc in next ch, sk next 2 chs, 5 dc in next ch—shell made; rep from * to last 3 chs; sk next 2 chs, dc in last ch, turn. *(29 [33, 37, 41] shells)*

Row 2: Ch 2 *(counts as a dc on this and following rows);* *sk next 2 dc, shell in next dc; sk next 2 dc, dc in next dc; rep from * to last shell; sk next 2 dc, shell in next dc; sk next 2 dc, dc in next ch of beg 6 sk chs, turn.

Row 3: Ch 2; *sk next 2 dc, shell in next dc; sk next 2 dc, dc in next dc; rep from * to last shell; sk next 2 dc, shell in next dc; sk next 2 dc, dc in 2nd ch of turning ch-2, turn.

Rows 3–16: Rep row 3. At end of row 16, change to A by drawing lp through; cut B.

Upper Body

Note: *On following rows, chs count as sts.*

Row 1: Ch 3 *(counts as a dc on this and following rows);* dc in next 5 dc; *ch 1, sk next dc, dc in next 5 dc; rep from * to turning ch-2; dc in 2nd ch of turning ch, turn. *(175 [199, 223, 247] sts)*

Row 2: Ch 3, dc in next 5 dc; *ch 1, dc in next 5 dc; rep from * to turning ch-3; dc in 3rd ch of turning ch-3, turn.

Rows 5–8: Rep row 2.

Right Front

For Size Small Only

Row 1: Ch 3, dc in next 5 dc, [ch 1, dc in next 5 dc] 5 times; dc in next ch-1 sp, turn, leaving rem sts unworked. *(37 sts)*

Row 2: Ch 3, dc in next 5 dc, [ch 1, dc in next 5 dc] 5 times; dc in 3rd ch of turning ch-3, turn.

Row 3: Ch 3, dc in next 5 dc, [ch 1, dc in next 5 dc] 5 times; dc in 3rd ch of turning ch-3, turn.

Rep rows 2 and 3 until armhole measures 8 inches. Fasten off.

Continue with Back.

For Size Medium Only

Row 1: Ch 3, dc in next 5 dc, [ch 1, dc in next 5 dc] 5 times; ch 1, dc in next 4 dc, turn, leaving rem sts unworked. *(41 sts)*

Row 2: Ch 3, dc in next 3 dc, [ch 1, dc in next 5 dc] 6 times; dc in 3rd ch of turning ch-3, turn.

Row 3: Ch 3, dc in next 5 dc, [ch 1, dc in next 5 dc] 5 times; ch 1, dc in next 3 dc and in 3rd ch of turning ch-3, turn.

Rep rows 2 and 3 until armhole measures 8½ inches. Fasten off.

Continue with Back.

For Size Large Only

Row 1: Ch 3, dc in next 5 dc, [ch 1, dc in next 5 dc] 6 times, turn, leaving rem sts unworked. *(42 sts)*

Row 2: Ch 3, dc in next 4 dc, [ch 1, dc in next 5 dc] 6 times; dc in 3rd ch of turning ch-3, turn.

Row 3: Ch 3, dc in next 5 dc, [ch 1, dc in next 5 dc] 6 times, turn.

Rep rows 2 and 3 until armhole measures 9 inches. Fasten off.

Continue with Back.

For Size X-Large Only

Row 1: Ch 3, dc in next 5 dc, [ch 1, dc in next 5 dc] 6 times; ch 1, dc in next 2 dc, turn, leaving rem sts unworked. *(45 sts)*

Row 2: Ch 3, dc in next dc, [ch 1, dc in next 5 dc] 7 times; dc in 3rd ch of turning ch-3, turn.

Row 3: Ch 3, dc in next 5 dc, [ch 1, dc in next 5 dc] 6 times; ch 1, dc in next dc and in 3rd ch of turning ch-3, turn.

Rep rows 2 and 3 until armhole measures 9½ inches. Fasten off.

Continue with Back.

Back

Hold piece with RS facing you; sk next 13 [18, 27, 33] unused sts from Right Front; join A in next st.

For Size Small Only

Row 1: Ch 3, dc in next 3 dc, [ch 1, dc in next 5 dc] 11 times; ch 1, dc in next 4 dc, turn, leaving rem sts unworked. *(75 sts)*

Row 2: Ch 3, dc in next 3 dc, [ch 1, dc in next 5 dc] 11 times; ch 1, dc in next 3 dc and in 3rd ch of beg ch-3.

Row 3: Ch 3, dc in next 3 dc, [ch 1, dc in next 5 dc] 11 times; ch 1, dc in next 3 dc and in 3rd ch of turning ch-3.

Rep row 3 until piece measures same as Right Front.

Continue with Left Front.

For Size Medium Only

Row 1: Ch 4 *(counts as a dc and a ch-1 sp on this and following rows),* dc in next 5 dc, [ch 1, dc in next 5 dc] 12 times; ch 1, dc in next dc, turn, leaving rem sts unworked. *(81 sts)*

Row 2: Ch 4, dc in next 5 dc, [ch 1, dc in next 5 dc] 12 times; ch 1, dc in 3rd ch of beg ch-4.

Row 3: Ch 4, dc in next 5 dc, [ch 1, dc in next 5 dc] 12 times; ch 1, dc in 3rd ch of turning ch-4.

Rep row 3 until piece measures same as Right Front.

Continue with Left Front.

For Size Large Only

Row 1: Ch 3, dc in next 2 dc, [ch 1, dc in next 5 dc] 13 times; ch 1, dc in next 3 dc, turn, leaving rem sts unworked. *(85 sts)*

Row 2: Ch 3, dc in next 2 dc, [ch 1, dc in next 5 dc] 13 times; ch 1, dc in next 2 dc and in 3rd ch of beg ch-3.

Row 3: Ch 3, dc in next 2 dc, [ch 1, dc in next 5 dc] 13 times; ch 1, dc in next 2 dc and in 3rd ch of turning ch-3.

Rep row 3 until piece measures same as Right Front.

Continue with Left Front.

For Size X-Large Only

Row 1: Ch 3, dc in next 5 dc, [ch 1, dc in next 5 dc] 14 times; dc in next dc, turn, leaving rem sts unworked. *(91 sts)*

Row 2: Ch 3, dc in next 5 dc, [ch 1, dc in next 5 dc] 14 times; dc in 3rd ch of beg ch-3.

Row 3: Ch 3, dc in next 5 dc, [ch 1, dc in next 5 dc] 14 times; dc in 3rd ch of turning ch-3.

Rep row 3 until piece measures same as Right Front.

Continue with Left Front.

Left Front

Hold piece with RS facing you; sk next 13 [18, 27, 33] unused sts from Back; join A in next st.

For Small Size Only

Row 1: Ch 3, dc in next 5 dc, [ch 1, dc in next 5 dc] 5 times; dc in 3rd ch of turning ch-3, turn. *(37 sts)*

Row 2: Ch 3, dc in next 5 dc, [ch 1, dc in next 5 dc] 5 times; dc in 3rd ch of beg ch-3, turn.

Row 3: Ch 3, dc in next 5 dc, [ch 1, dc in next 5 dc] 5 times; dc in 3rd ch of turning ch-3, turn.

Rep row 3 until armhole measures 8 inches. Fasten off.

Continue with Sleeve.

For Size Medium Only

Row 1: Ch 3, dc in next 3 dc, [ch 1, dc in next 5 dc] 5 times; ch 1, dc in next 5 dc and in 3rd ch of turning ch-3, turn. *(41 sts)*

Row 2: Ch 3, dc in next 5 dc, [ch 1, dc in next 5 dc] 5 times; ch 1, dc in next 3 dc and in 3rd ch of beg ch-3, turn.

Row 3: Ch 3, dc in next 3 dc, [ch 1, dc in next 5 dc] 5 times; ch 1, dc in next 5 dc and in 3rd ch of turning ch-3, turn.

Row 4: Ch 3, dc in next 5 dc, [ch 1, dc in next 5 dc] 5 times; ch 1, dc in next 3 dc and in 3rd ch of turning ch-3, turn.

Row 5: Ch 3, dc in next 3 dc, [ch 1, dc in next 5 dc] 5 times; ch 1, dc in next 5 dc and in 3rd ch of turning ch-3, turn.

Rep rows 4 and 5 until armhole measures 8½ inches. Fasten off.

Continue with Sleeve.

For Size Large Only

Row 1: Ch 3, dc in next 4 dc, [ch 1, dc in next 5 dc] 6 times; dc in 3rd ch of turning ch-3, turn. *(42 sts)*

Row 2: Ch 3, dc in next 5 dc, [ch 1, dc in next 5 dc] 5 times; ch 1, dc next 4 dc and in 3rd ch of beg ch-3, turn.

Row 3: Ch 3, dc in next 4 dc, [ch 1, dc in next 5 dc] 6 times; dc in 3rd ch of turning ch-3, turn.

Row 4: Ch 3, dc in next 5 dc, [ch 1, dc in next 5 dc] 5 times; ch 1, dc next 4 dc and in 3rd ch of turning ch-3, turn.

Row 5: Ch 3, dc in next 4 dc, [ch 1, dc in next 5 dc] 6 times; dc in 3rd ch of turning ch-3, turn.

Rep rows 4 and 5 until armhole measures 9 inches. Fasten off.

Continue with Sleeve.

For Size X-Large Only

Row 1: Ch 3, dc in next dc, [ch 1, dc in next 5 dc] 7 times; dc in 3rd ch of turning ch-3, turn. *(45 sts)*

Row 2: Ch 3, dc in next 5 dc, [ch 1, dc in next 5 dc] 6 times; ch 1, dc in next dc and in 3rd ch of beg ch-3, turn.

Row 3: Ch 3, dc in next dc; [ch 1, dc in next 5 dc] 7 times; dc in 3rd ch of turning ch-3, turn.

Row 4: Ch 3, dc in next 5 dc, [ch 1, dc in next 5 dc] 6 times; ch 1, dc in next dc and in 3rd ch of turning ch-3, turn.

Row 5: Ch 3, dc in next dc; [ch 1, dc in next 5 dc] 7 times; dc in 3rd ch of turning ch-3, turn.

Rep rows 4 and 5 until armhole measures 9½ inches. Fasten off.

Continue with Sleeve.

Sleeve

For Sizes Small & Large Only

Row 1 (RS): With D hook and A, ch 75 [85]; dc in 4th ch from hook *(beg 3 sk chs count as a dc)* and in next 4 chs; *ch 1, sk next ch, dc in next 5 chs; rep from * to last ch; dc in last ch, turn. *(73 [83] sts)*

Row 2: Ch 3 *(counts as a dc on this and following rows),* dc in first dc; *dc in next 5 dc, ch 1; rep from * to last 5 dc and beg 3 sk chs; dc in last 5 dc, 2 dc in 3rd ch of beg 3 sk chs, turn. *(75 [85] sts)*

Row 3: Ch 3, dc in first dc, ch 1, sk next dc; *dc in next 5 dc, ch 1; rep from * to last 6 dc and turning ch-3; dc in last 5 dc, ch 1, sk next dc, 2 dc in 3rd ch of turning ch-3, turn. *(77 [87] sts)*

Row 4: Ch 3, dc in first dc and in next dc; *ch 1, dc in next 5 dc; rep from * to last ch-1 sp; ch 1, dc in next dc, 2 dc in 3rd ch of turning ch-3, turn. *(79 [89] sts)*

Row 5: Ch 3, dc in first dc and in next 2 dc; *ch 1, dc in next 5 dc; rep from * to last ch-1 sp; ch 1, dc in next 2 dc, 2 dc in 3rd ch of turning ch-3, turn. *(81 [91] sts)*

Row 6: Ch 3, dc in first dc and in next 3 dc; *ch 1, dc in next 5 dc; rep from * to last ch-1 sp; ch 1, dc in next 3 dc, 2 dc in 3rd ch of turning ch-3, turn. *(83 [93] sts)*

Row 7: Ch 3, dc in first dc and in next 4 dc; *ch 1, dc in next 5 dc; rep from * to last ch-1 sp; ch 1, dc in next 4 dc, 2 dc in 3rd ch of turning ch-3, turn. *(85 [95] sts)*

Row 8: Ch 3, dc in next 5 dc; *ch 1, dc in next 5 dc; rep from * to turning ch-3; dc in 3rd ch of turning ch-3, turn.

Rows 9 & 10: Rep row 8.

Fasten off and weave in ends.

Continue with Assembly.

For Sizes Medium & X-Large Only

Row 1 (RS): With D hook and A, ch [81, 91]; dc in 4th ch from hook *(beg 3 sk chs count as a dc)* and in next ch; *ch 1, sk next ch, dc in next 5 chs; rep from * to last 4 chs; ch 1, sk next ch, dc in last 3 chs, turn. *([79, 89] sts)*

Row 2: Ch 3 *(counts as a dc on this and following rows),* dc in first dc and in next 2 dc; *ch 1, dc in next 5 dc; rep from * to last ch-1 sp; ch 1, dc in next 2 dc, 2 dc in 3rd ch of beg 3 sk chs, turn. *([81, 91] sts)*

Row 3: Ch 3, dc in first dc and in next 3 dc; *ch 1, dc in next 5 dc; rep from * to last ch-1 sp; ch 1, dc in next 3 dc, 2 dc in 3rd ch of turning ch-3, turn. *([83, 93] sts)*

Row 4: Ch 3, dc in first dc and in next 4 dc; *ch 1, dc in next 5 dc; rep from * to last ch-1 sp; ch 1, dc in next 4 dc, 2 dc in 3rd ch of turning ch-3, turn. *([85, 95] sts)*

Row 5: Ch 3, dc in first dc and in next 5 dc; *ch 1, dc in next 5 dc; rep from * to last ch-1 sp; ch 1, dc in next 5 dc, 2 dc in 3rd ch of turning ch-3, turn. *([87, 97] sts)*

Row 6: Ch 3, dc in first dc, ch 1, sk next dc, dc in next 5 dc; *ch 1, dc in next 5 dc; rep from * to last ch-1 sp; ch 1, dc in next 5 dc, ch 1, sk next dc, 2 dc in 3rd ch of turning ch-3, turn. *([89, 99] sts)*

Row 7: Ch 3, dc in first dc and in next dc; *ch 1, dc in next 5 dc; rep from * to last ch-1 sp; ch 1, dc in next dc, 2 dc in 3rd ch of turning ch-3, turn. *([91, 101] sts)*

Row 8: Ch 3, dc in next 2 dc; *ch 1, dc in next 5 dc; rep from * to last ch-1 sp; ch 1, dc in next 2 dc and in 3rd ch of turning ch-3, turn.

Rows 9 & 10: Rep row 8.

Fasten off and weave in ends.

Continue with Assembly.

Assembly

Sew shoulder seams. Sew seam in Sleeves from rows 1–7. Sew Sleeves to jacket.

Edgings

Neck Edging

Hold jacket with WS facing you; with D hook, join B in first st at top of Left Front.

Row 1 (WS): Ch 1, sc in same st and in each st across Left Front; sc in seam and in each dc across Back; sc in next seam and in each st across Right Front, turn.

Row 2 (RS): Ch 3; *sk next 2 sc, 5 dc in next sc; sk next 2 sc, dc in next sc; rep from * across, adjusting last rep to have last dc in last sc, turn.

Row 3: Ch 3; *sk next 2 dc, 7 dc in next dc, sk next 2 dc, dc in next dc; rep from * once more; sk next 2 dc, 7 dc in next dc; sk next 2 dc, sl st in next dc. Fasten off. Sk back sts, and rejoin crochet cotton to dc before 3rd 5-dc group from front edge; **sk next 2 dc, 7 dc in next dc; sk next 2 dc, dc in next dc; rep from ** twice more. Fasten off.

Sleeve Edging

With D hook, join A in 1 sleeve seam; ch 1, sc in same sp and in each st; join in first sc. Fasten off.

Rep on other sleeve.

Lower Edging

Hold jacket with RS facing you and beg ch at top; with D hook, join A in unused lp of first ch of beg ch; ch 3, sk next 2 chs, in next unused lp work [tr, ch 3, sl st in top of tr just made] 6 times; tr in same lp; sk next 2 chs, sc in next unused lp; rep from * across.

Fasten off and weave in all ends.

Tie

Make 2.

Hold jacket with RS facing you; with D hook, join B to Right Front about 6 inches down from last A row; make a ch 12 inches in length. Fasten off and weave in ends. Tie charm to end of tie with double knot.

Rep on Left Front of jacket.

Quick Accent Scarf

Size

About 3 x 53 inches

Materials

- J. & P. Coats Royale size 3 crochet cotton: 150 yds #264 lime
- Size E/4/3.5mm crochet hook
- Tapestry needle

Gauge

Gauge not important for this project.

Instructions

Center

Rnd 1: Ch 5, join with a tr to form a ring; ch 5, [tr in ring, ch 1] 6 times; tr in ring, ch 5, sl st in ring, turn.

Rnd 2: Ch 5, in first ch-5 sp work [tr, ch 1] 7 times; tr in same sp, ch 5, sl st in next ch-1 sp, turn.

Rep rnd 2 until piece measures about 53 inches in length.

Edging

Ch 1, sc in same ch-1 sp as last sl st made, ch 3; *[sc in next ch-1 sp, ch 3] 5 times; in next ch-5 sp work [sc, ch 3] 3 times; rep from * to beg ring; in beg ring work [sc, ch 3] twice; **[sc in next ch-1 sp, ch 3] 6 times; in next ch-5 sp work [sc, ch 3] twice; rep from ** to first sc; join in first sc.

Fasten off and weave in ends.

How to Check Gauge

A correct stitch gauge is very important. Please take the time to work a stitch gauge swatch about 4 x 4 inches. Measure the swatch. If the number of stitches and rows are fewer than indicated under "Gauge" in the pattern, your hook is too large. Try another swatch with a smaller size hook. If the number of stitches and rows are more than indicated under "Gauge" in the pattern, your hook is too small. Try another swatch with a larger size hook.

Abbreviations & Symbols

beg .... begin/beginning
bpdc .... back post double crochet
bpsc .... back post single crochet
bptr .... back post treble crochet
CC .... contrasting color
ch .... chain stitch
ch- .... refers to chain or space previously made (i.e. ch-1 space)
ch sp .... chain space
cl .... cluster
cm .... centimeter(s)
dc .... double crochet
dc dec .... double crochet 2 or more stitches together, as indicated
dec .... decrease/decreases/decreasing
dtr .... double treble crochet
fpdc .... front post double crochet
fpsc .... front post single crochet
fptr .... front post treble crochet
g .... grams
hdc .... half double crochet
hdc dec ... half double crochet 2 or more stitches together, as indicated
lp(s) .... loops(s)
MC .... main color
mm .... millimeter(s)
oz .... ounce(s)
pc .... popcorn
rem .... remain/remaining
rep .... repeat(s)
rnd(s) .... round(s)
RS .... right side
sc .... single crochet
sc dec .... single crochet 2 or more stitches together, as indicated
sk .... skip
sl st .... slip stitch
sp(s) .... space(s)
st(s) .... stitch(es)
tog .... together
tr .... treble crochet
trtr .... triple treble
WS .... wrong side
yd(s) .... yard(s)
yo .... yarn over

* An asterisk (or double asterisk **) is used to mark the beginning of a portion of instructions to be worked more than once; thus, "rep from * twice more" means after working the instructions once, repeat the instructions following the asterisk twice more (3 times in all).

[] Brackets are used to enclose instructions that should be worked the exact number of times specified immediately following the brackets, such as "[2 sc in next dc, sc in next dc] twice." They are also used to set off and clarify a group of stitches that are to be worked all into the same space or stitch, such as "in next corner sp work [2 dc, ch 1, 2 dc]."

[] Brackets and () parentheses are used to provide additional information to clarify instructions.

Join—join with a sl st unless otherwise specified.

The patterns in this book are written using United States terminology. Terms that have different British equivalents are noted below.

U.S. Terms	U.K. Terms
single crochet (sc)	double crochet (dc)
double crochet (dc)	treble (tr)
treble crochet (tr)	double treble (dtr)
skip (sk)	miss
slip stitch (sl st)	slip stitch (ss) or single crochet
gauge	tension
yarn over (yo)	yarn over hook (YOH)

Stitch Guide

Chain—ch:
YO, draw through lp on hook.

Single Crochet—sc:
Insert hook in st, yo and draw through, yo and draw through both lps on hook.

Reverse Single Crochet—Reverse sc:
Work from left to right, insert hook in sp or st indicated (**a**), draw lp through sp or st - 2 lps on hook (**b**); yo and draw through lps on hook.

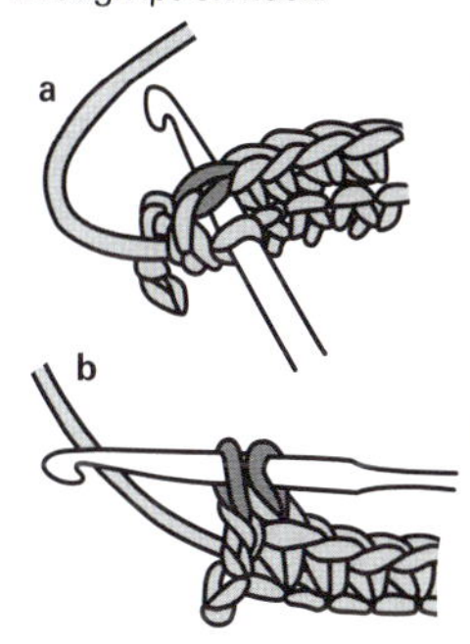

Half Double Crochet—hdc:
yo, insert hook in st, yo, draw through, yo and draw through all 3 lps on hook.

Double Crochet—dc:
yo, insert hook in st, yo, draw through, (yo and draw through 2 lps on hook) twice.

Triple Crochet—trc:
yo twice, insert hook in st, yo, draw through, (yo and draw through 2 lps on hook) 3 times.

Slip Stitch—sl st:
(**a**) **Used for Joinings**
Insert hook in indicated st, yo and draw through st and lp on hook.

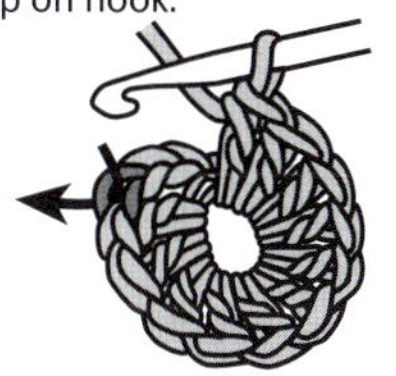

(**b**) **Used for Moving Yarn Over**
Insert hook in st, yo draw through st and lp on hook.

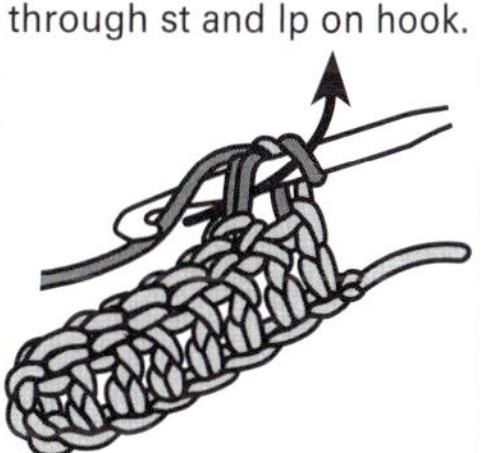

Front Loop—FL:
The front loop is the loop toward you at the top of the stitch.

Back Loop—BL:
The back loop is the loop away from you at the top of the stitch.

Post:
The post is the vertical part of the stitch.

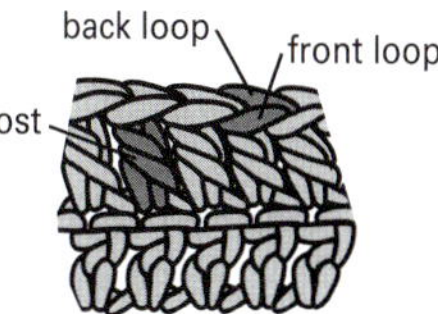

Overcast Stitch is worked loosely to join crochet pieces.

Skill Levels

BEGINNER
Beginner projects for first-time crocheters using basic stitches. Minimal shaping.

EASY
Easy projects using basic stitches, repetitive stitch patterns, simple color changes and simple shaping and finishing.

INTERMEDIATE
Intermediate projects with a variety of stitches, mid-level shaping and finishing.

EXPERIENCED
Experienced projects using advanced techniques and stitches, detailed shaping and refined finishing.

Standard Yarn Weight System

Categories of yarn, gauge ranges, and recommended needle and hook sizes

Yarn Weight Symbol & Category Names	1 SUPER FINE	2 FINE	3 LIGHT	4 MEDIUM	5 BULKY	6 SUPER BULKY
Type of Yarns in Category	Sock, Fingering, Baby	Sport, Baby	DK, Light Worsted	Worsted, Afghan, Aran	Chunky, Craft, Rug	Bulky, Roving
Crochet Gauge* Ranges in Single Crochet to 4 inch	21–32 sts	16–20 sts	12–17 sts	11–14 sts	8–11 sts	5–9 sts
Recommended Hook in Metric Size Range	2.25–3.5 mm	3.5–4.5 mm	4.5–5.5 mm	5.5–6.5 mm	6.5–9 mm	9 mm and larger
Recommended Hook U.S. Size Range	B1–E4	E4–7	7–I-9	I-9–K-10½	K-10½–M-13	M-13 and larger

* GUIDELINES ONLY: The above reflect the most commonly used gauges and hook sizes for specific yarn categories.

Metric Chart

CROCHET HOOKS CONVERSION CHART

U.S.	1/B	2/C	3/D	4/E	5/F	6/G	8/H	9/I	10/J	10½/K	N
Continental-mm	2.25	2.75	3.25	3.5	3.75	4.25	5	5.5	6	6.5	9.0

DRG Publishing
306 East Parr Road
Berne, IN 46711

TOLL-FREE ORDER LINE or to request a free catalog (800) 582-6643
Customer Service (800) 282-6643, **Fax** (800) 882-6643

Visit AnniesAttic.com.

ISBN:1-59012-156-2 Printed in USA 1 2 3 4 5 6 7 8 9